Contents

Any words appearing in bold, **like this**, are explained in the Glossary.

What a lot of rot!

What happens to old, dead plants and animals? They lie around on the ground – but not for long. Over time they go mouldy and rotten, turning into crumbly pieces or smelly goo. Finally they break into tiny bits too small to see, which go into the soil. This whole process is called rotting or **decay**.

This old log is slowly rotting into the soil. Millions of living things, from worms and **grubs** to tiny bugs, are making it rot.

This tiny rotter is called a roundworm. It would fit onto the full stop at the end of this sentence. A microscope shows it as larger than a finger.

The micro-rotters

Rotting is done by living things. Many 'rotters' are so tiny that we need a magnifying glass, or even a **microscope**, to see them. This book tells the story of the micro-rotters. Their world is dirty and smelly – but we need them. Without them we would be knee-deep in old bits of plants and animals, which have not rotted away.

A heap of rotters

In a huge jungle there are many kinds of animals, from mice and monkeys to tigers and elephants. When we put old leaves, grass and leftover food on a **compost heap**, we make a 'mini-jungle'. Many creatures live in a compost heap, but most are too small to see. Some munch bits of plants while others are fierce hunters.

Many people put old leaves, twigs and other garden material on to a compost heap. This helps natural recycling.

WHAT DOES NOT ROT
Substances we make in factories, such as glass, metal and plastic, do not rot. They last for thousands of years. So we should put them in recycling bins so they can be used again.

Back to soil

In a compost heap, tiny animals and other microlife gradually turn once-living things into soil. The soil is rich in food for growing new plants. Rotting is nature's way of using things again and again. It is natural recycling.

Micro-rotters include frilly- and tube-shaped **bacteria**.

The rot sets in

When old things start to rot, minibeasts soon move in. They chew and chomp as they feed. They break up soft things such as flowers and fruits very quickly. Hard pieces such as bark and wood take longer. But minibeasts never stop nibbling.

WOODWORM

Sometimes small, worm-like grubs, called woodworm, eat wood in houses and furniture. Then they turn into beetles, come out of the wood and fly away. They leave small holes in the wood where they come out.

As beetle grubs eat wood, they leave a pattern of tunnels.

Woodlice chew damp wood and soon turn it into a soft powder.

Munching minibeasts

Minibeast rotters include earwigs, woodlice, millipedes, as well as the **grubs** (young) of beetles, ants and other insects. As they eat, pieces of food fall out of their mouths – like the crumbs when we eat cake and biscuits. These pieces do not go to waste. They are food for even smaller rotters!

Nests for rotters

Termites and some ants eat old wood with their tiny, pincer-like mouths. They make tunnels and nests inside the wood. Termites and ants can chew through wooden furniture, houses and even bridges, until they collapse in a heap of powder.

Termites scurry through their tunnels, chewing bits of rotting wood.

This building has been destroyed by termites.

Mouldy food

Other termites and ants make nests in soil. They take old leaves, twigs, flowers and small dead animals to the nest. As these things become **mouldy** and rotten, the termites and ants feed on them.

LOTS OF EGGS
Only one termite in a nest lays eggs – the queen. She can lay 1000 eggs every day for ten years!

Rotten meat

Animals die all the time. Fish and frogs, elephants and eagles – no creature lives for ever. When a creature dies, the rotters move in. Flies lay their eggs on the dead body. The eggs quickly hatch into **maggots**, which eat into the rotting flesh. Beetles lay their eggs too. Out of the eggs hatch **grubs**.

KEEP FOOD CLEAN
Flies spread micro-rotters and germs on to our food. We should keep our meat covered and clean, and make sure it is properly cooked.

Maggots have no eyes, legs or feelers. They turn into adult flies.

Meat and bones

As maggots and grubs eat, they leave behind bits of half-chewed meat. They also leave droppings. These droppings are food for more rotters. Soon the dead animal's body is mostly **decayed** and gone, with just the hard bones left behind. Even these bones crumble into the soil after a long time.

The body of this warthog (a type of wild pig) is gradually rotting into the mud.

Waste not, want not

Animals do not use toilets. They leave their waste droppings, or dung, on the ground. Droppings smell horrible to us. But they smell wonderful to many tiny creatures, such as flies and beetles. These mini-rotters rush to the fresh piles of droppings and eat them!

The dung beetle rolls dung into a ball and lays eggs on it. When the grubs hatch they eat the dung.

PLENTY OF DUNG
One elephant produces over 120 kilograms (265 pounds) of droppings every day. That is the weight of two adult people – and enough to feed 3000 dung beetles!

Piles of fresh dung such as cow pats are food for hungry flies and beetles.

A smelly meal

Droppings contain bits of leftover food. So mini-rotters have a great feast. Some kinds of flies and beetles lay their eggs on the droppings. The eggs hatch into **maggots** and **grubs**, which also feed on the smelly meal. Soon the droppings are broken up and are gone.

Mite decay

A bucketful of soil contains thousands of **mites**. Mites are tiny, eight-legged cousins of spiders. They chew the munched-up leftovers from bigger creatures, including bits of old leaves, flowers, fruits and twigs. As they feed, they make even smaller leftovers, which help the rot and **decay**.

MITES EAT MITES! Many kinds of mites eat old, rotting bits of plants and animals. But they are always in danger – from other kinds of mites, which try to eat them!

Millions of mites live in the layer of needle leaves under **conifer** trees such as pines and firs.

Turtle mites have hard, rounded shells, like a turtle's shell.

Cool and damp

Most mites live in **leaf litter**. This is the layer of dead leaves and other bits on top of soil. One old leaf might have 1000 tiny mites chewing it to bits. Mites like to feed when the weather is cool and damp. When the sun comes out, they crawl down into the soil. They will die if they get too warm and dry.

Wriggly rotters

Some of the best rotters are worms. There are many different kinds of worms. Big earthworms can grow as long as a person's arm. Some roundworms, or nematodes, are too small to see. Most of these worms eat almost any dead thing they can find. Some worms wriggle through soil while others burrow into dead animals and plants.

An earthworm has no eyes or ears at its head end – just a round mouth that swallows tiny pieces of soil.

LONGEST WORMS

Ribbonworms live on the seashore. They scavenge (eat dead parts of animals). They are the longest worms. Some are more than 30 metres long!

This roundworm lives in the sea. It searches for dead fish and other water creatures to eat.

Rotters in water

Rotting does not only happen in soil and **compost heaps**. It also happens on the bottom of ponds, rivers, lakes and the sea. Water-living worms burrow into the bodies of dead creatures such as fish and even whales, and eat them to pieces.

19

Living by rotting

Moulds can grow almost anywhere. If you leave fruit for too long in a bowl, it goes **mouldy**. Even vegetables on a shelf, clothes in a damp cupboard, and damp paper can go mouldy.

This fruit has gone rotten from the middle outwards. The rings on its skin are called pinmoulds.

Moulds grow on the plaster on damp walls and ceilings, forming dark patches.

Old and mouldy

Moulds are living things called **fungi**. All fungi live by rotting plant or animal material. They get their food by making special substances that eat into living or dead things, turning them into a liquid. The hungry fungus then soaks up this liquid. As the fungus does this, it speeds rot and **decay**. There are thousands of kinds of fungi. You can read more about them on the next page.

LOTS OF NAMES

There are lots of names for different kinds of fungi. There are moulds, pinmoulds, mildews, rusts, blights, yeasts, mushrooms, toadstools and lots more!

Threads of decay

Moulds and other **fungi** cause most of the world's rotting. They make dead things rot until there is nothing left. They do this by growing tiny threads, which are usually too thin to see. The threads eat their way into dead bits of plants and animals. Then the threads turn them into a liquid, and soak it up as food.

Dry rot is a fungus that grows through wood. It makes the wood **decay** into a powder.

LOTS OF THREADS
If you could take all the threads of a fungus from a cupful of soil, and join them end to end, they could stretch more than 100 metres.

The threads of a fungus form a tangled net in the soil, like a spider's web.

Killer fungi

Some kinds of fungi spread through the soil. If their threads touch an old leaf or an animal dropping, they grow around it and into it, and rot it. Sometimes they grow into living things, such as trees, flowers or sick animals, and do the same. This is when fungi are not only rotters – they are killers, too.

Spreading the rot

Fungi are the world's best rotters. This is partly because they spread themselves so fast. The main part of a fungus is its tangled net of tiny threads. But in some places, the threads grow into larger parts, called fruiting bodies. In many kinds of fungus, these are quite big. We call the fruiting bodies mushrooms or toadstools.

A mushroom releases its spores from ridges, called gills, under its cap.

One spore from a fungus is too small to see. But millions together look like a powdery cloud, floating away from this earthstar fungus.

How fungi spread

Mushrooms and toadstools can be bigger than a dinner plate or smaller than a pin's head. They make seed-like **spores**, which are far too small to see. The spores float away in the wind. If the spores land in a suitable damp place, they grow into new fungi. This is how fungi spread.

PUFF, PUFF
A puffball is a round fungus, the size of a soccer ball. It can puff out as many as 20,000 million tiny spores!

As things rot, they break into smaller pieces, which are eaten by tinier creatures. Smallest of all are two kinds of microlife – protists and **bacteria**. Protists are jelly-like blobs that slide along, taking in any bits of food. Bacteria are even smaller living things – about 1000 would fit on the dot of this 'i'. They soak up almost any kind of juicy rotten food.

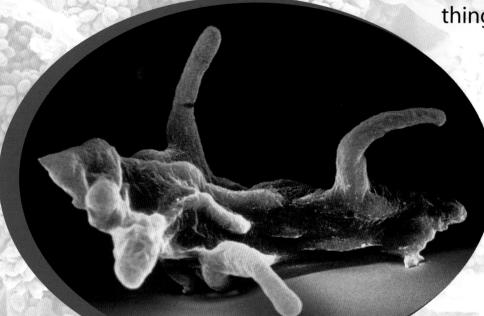

This kind of protist is called an amoeba. It has lots of bendy arms, which wave about to catch tiny pieces of food.

ROTTERS WE EAT
People can eat some fungi, from ordinary mushrooms to potato-shaped **truffles**. But other fungi are poisonous. We must be sure which kind they are.

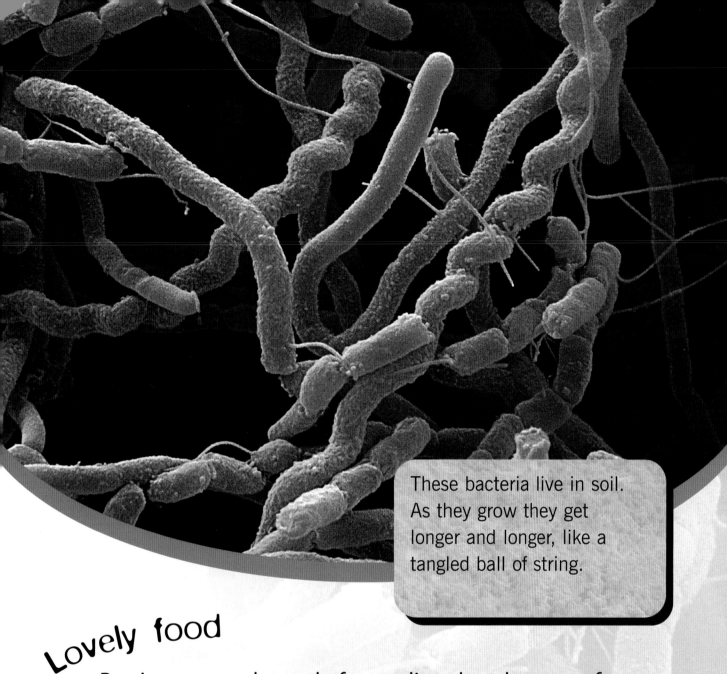

These bacteria live in soil. As they grow they get longer and longer, like a tangled ball of string.

Lovely food

Rotting means the end of some lives, but the start of others. Tiny bacteria, protists, **fungi** and minibeasts get their food from making other things rot. Then they become food, too. These rotters are eaten by centipedes, spiders and many other animals. In turn, these small animals are eaten by larger animals. This is how rotting becomes nature's way of recycling.

Stop the rot!

Rotting can ruin our farm crops, fruits, vegetables and meat. It can also damage the wood in our furniture and houses. Rot happens faster in warm and damp places. To try to stop things rotting, we keep them cool and dry. Refrigerators slow down rot, because they are cold. Freezers can almost stop it completely.

If our foods stay too warm and damp, like these lettuces, they soon go **mouldy**.

Why we need rot

People try to stop rot in some places. But in nature, rot is very important. It gets rid of old, dead plants and animals. It recycles (reuses) their tiniest parts into soil. Then new plants can grow and animals can eat the plants. We all depend on microlife that rots things.

CLEANING AWAY ROTTERS

Keeping things clean and dry helps to stop **decay**. It removes the tiny **spores** of **fungi** and other rotters, which float in air and hide in dirt.

Chemicals called **fungicides** stop moulds growing. Farmers sometimes spray their crops with them.

Find out for yourself

Books to read

A Handful of Dirt, Raymond Bial (Illustrator) (Walker & Company, 2000)

A Log's Life, E. Wendy Pfeffer and Robin Brickman (Illustrator) (Simon & Schuster Children's Publishing, 1997)

Compost, By Gosh!, Michelle Eva Portman (Flower Press, 2002)

Inside Guides: Microlife, David Burnie (Dorling Kindersley Family Library, 1997)

The Things in Mouldy Manor (A Mini Spooky Pop-up Book), Keith Moseley and Andy Everitt-Stewart (Grosset & Dunlap, 1994)

Using the internet

Explore the Internet to find out more about microlife that rots things. Websites can change, so if the links below no longer work, do not worry. Use a search engine, such as **www.yahooligans.com** or **www.internet4kids.com**, and type in a keyword such as fungus, mould, termite or compost, or the name of a particular type of microlife.

Websites

www.commtechlab.msu.edu/sites/dlc-me/zoo/zdcmain.html
Part of the Microbe Zoo Dirtland site explains about compost piles and what lives in them.

www.cornwallwildlifetrust.org.uk/educate/activity/decay.htm
Project ideas to study if different items and materials decay, and how fast they do so.

Disclaimer
All the Internet addresses (URLs) given in this book were valid at the time of going to press. However, due to the dynamic nature of the Internet, some addresses may have changed or ceased to exist since publication. While the author and publisher regret any inconvenience this may cause readers, no responsibility for any such changes can be accepted by either the author or the publisher.

Glossary

bacteria tiny living things. Some bacteriamake things rot.

compost heap pile of dead plant material such as leaves, grass cuttings and vegetable peelings

conifer type of tree that grows cones rather than flowers, such as a pine or fir tree

decay break apart and go rotten or mouldy

fungi group of living things including mushrooms, toadstools and yeasts. Fungi cause rotting.

fungicides substances that kill fungi

grub a baby beetle that looks like a worm

leaf litter mixture of dead leaves, bits of twigs and loose soil found under trees

maggot young or larva of a fly. Maggots do not have legs.

microscope equipment to make very small things look bigger

mite small eight-legged creature. Some mites cause disease and some are harmless to people.

mouldy going bad or rotten due to mould, a type of fungus

spores tiny, seed-like parts that are made by fungi. Spores grow into new fungi.

truffle type of potato-shaped fungi that grows underground

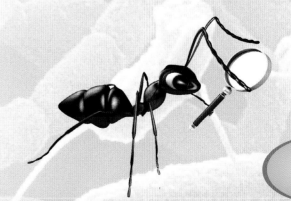

Index